Shelby the Snow Dog
A True Story

Written and Illustrated by Edith Richmond

Some names and identifying details have been changed to protect the privacy of individuals.

Copyright © 2024 by Edith Richmond

All rights reserved. No part of this book may be reproduced or transmitted in any form or by any means, electronic or mechanical, including photocopying, recording, or any information storage and retrieval system, without permission in writing from the author.

ISBN: 978-1-6653-0695-9 - Paperback
ISBN: 978-1-6653-0696-6 - Hardcover

These ISBNs are the property of BookLogix for the express purpose of sales and distribution of this title. The content of this book is the property of the copyright holder only. BookLogix does not hold any ownership of the content of this book and is not liable in any way for the materials contained within. The views and opinions expressed in this book are the property of the Author/Copyright holder, and do not necessarily reflect those of BookLogix.

Library of Congress Control Number: 2024908707

0 4 2 9 2 4

♾This paper meets the requirements of ANSI/NISO Z39.48-1992 (Permanence of Paper)

10

Shelby was my dog for about ten years. Not only was she stunningly beautiful, but she had a sunny personality as well. She was a joy to everyone who met her. Shelby howled a lot—she was great at expressing herself! She was truly a one-of-a-kind dog. I feel blessed to have been her owner.

Shelby is my Siberian husky. Siberian huskies come from a faraway land called Siberia. Deep snow, ice, and *fierce winds* are present throughout most of the year.

Long ago, the people hunted and gathered their food. They trained Siberian huskies to help them by pulling sleds loaded with supplies. Several huskies formed a team to do the work. Huskies are strong and love to **run**. Even today, husky teams pull sleds in snowy places.

Siberian huskies have two layers of fur. The outer layer protects the dog from snow and rain. Underneath is soft, thick, white fur that keeps them warm and dry during cold and windy weather.

One hot summer day,
I saw two beautiful Siberian
huskies walking down my street.
Then they came into my yard!
They were hot and thirsty.

I brought them many bowls of water.
They drank them all before lying under a shady tree to cool off.

Soon I found the dogs' owner, Ms. Tracy, who sold husky puppies. She was so excited to see her dogs and was grateful I had rescued them from the heat. She told me they were a sister and brother named Shelby and Romeo.

I visited Shelby and Romeo all the time.
Sometimes they would greet me by howling

wo, wo,

wo,

the sound huskies make
instead of barking. They
remembered me and the kindness
I had shown them on that hot
summer day.

One day, Ms. Tracy called me and asked if I would take Shelby because she didn't want to sell Siberian husky puppies anymore. From that day forward, Shelby was my devoted companion.

Wherever we go, people marvel at Shelby's beauty and friendliness.

On Saturdays, we walk to the rehab center. When I get out her leash, Shelby dances around, wags her big fluffy tail, and gives me a "husky howl." She's ready to go!

On our way, we see Casper, the neighborhood cat. He is big and black. He and Shelby are friends. Casper sits up and stretches while Shelby bends over to sniff him, wagging her tail.

Shelby watches the mailman deliver mail and packages to everyone's mailbox in the neighborhood. He always stops his truck to throw her a treat.

At the rehab center, the nurses are happy to see Shelby and me. They gather around to greet us. They know Shelby is a special dog who brings joy to everyone she meets.

Shelby is calm and quiet as we move from room to room visiting the residents. They pat her head and speak to her. She makes them smile because she is so pretty and sweet.

On our way home, we see Officer Mac and his police dog, Bronson. Together they make the neighborhood safe.

In spring, Shelby no longer needs her thick white undercoat. She sheds the white fur. Birds pick up pieces of Shelby's white fur to make a soft nest for their eggs.

In summer, thunderstorms arrive with the heat.
Shelby loves to stand in the rain.

In fall, Shelby plays in the leaves. The cooler weather makes Shelby's thick white undercoat grow in. Soon she'll be ready for winter *again*.

Shelby is a marvelous dog, **full** of energy and eager to please. She makes my life better with her beauty, loyalty, and companionship.

21

About the Author

Edith Richmond has spent most of her life in medicine. She worked many years as a respiratory therapist in the Neonatal Intensive Care Unit. She fosters dogs for Angels Among Us Pet Rescue. In addition, she is a published poet, and a proud grandmother.

This book is dedicated to Dr. David Lahasky
10% of the proceeds go to Angels Among Us Pet Rescue

Printed in the USA
CPSIA information can be obtained
at www.ICGtesting.com
CBHW061451110824
12966CB00048B/872